TEEN LIFE™

FREQUENTLY ASKED QUESTIONS ABOUT

Vaccines and Vaccinations

Christine
Petersen

New York

Published in 2011 by The Rosen Publishing Group, Inc.
29 East 21st Street, New York, NY 10010

Library of Congress Cataloging-in-Publication Data

Petersen, Christine.
Frequently asked questions about vaccines and vaccinations /
Christine Petersen.—1st ed.
    p. cm.—(FAQ: teen life)
Includes bibliographical references and index.
ISBN 978-1-4488-1328-5 (lib. bdg.)
1. Vaccines—Popular works. 2. Vaccination—Popular works.
I. Title.
RA638.P48 2011
615'.372—dc22

                                                    2010018499

Manufactured in the United States of America

CPSIA Compliance Information: Batch #W11YA: For further information, contact Rosen Publishing, New York, New York,
at 1-800-237-9932.

Contents

1

Why Were Vaccines
Developed? 4

2

Are Vaccines
Effective? 15

3

How Many Vaccines
Are There? 24

4

Do the Benefits of
Vaccination Outweigh
the Risks? 34

5

Should Vaccination
Be Mandatory? 46

Glossary 52
For More Information 54
For Further Reading 57
Bibliography 58
Index 62

one

WHY WERE VACCINES DEVELOPED?

The discovery of Egyptian tombs was a popular and exciting goal of science in the nineteenth century. Among the most fascinating was KV35, excavated in 1898 by French archaeologist Victor Loret. Inside the tomb, Loret found the remains of a once-powerful pharaoh named Amenhotep II, who ruled over Egypt's Valley of the Kings more than 3,400 years ago. But Amenhotep II was not alone.

Tucked in a side chamber of Amenhotep II's mazelike tomb were a dozen other mummies, apparently transferred from their original tombs as protection from grave robbers. Among them was Pharaoh Ramses V, a minor king who had ruled for only four years and died in 1157 BCE. An examination by archaeologist C. W. Dixon revealed that the pharaoh had been young at the time of his death—no older than forty. Noting a prominent rash on the mummy's head,

Smallpox has afflicted people for thousands of years. Scars on the body of mummified Egyptian pharaoh Ramses V, more than three thousand years old, provide one of the oldest records of this disease.

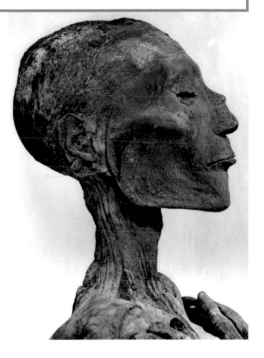

neck, and shoulders, Dixon reported that the pharaoh's untimely death had been caused by disease. Doctors Marc Armand Ruffer and A. R. Ferguson were curious to learn which illness had killed Ramses V. In 1911, they visited the mummy in a Cairo museum. After close study, Ruffer and Ferguson decided that the pattern of bubblelike marks on the three-thousand-year-old body "bore a striking resemblance to that of smallpox."

An Ancient Disease

Humans have always experienced disease. Malaria, cholera, plague, diphtheria, tuberculosis, typhoid fever, pneumonia, influenza . . . the list seems endless. Among all of these dreaded diseases, however, smallpox has left a wider path of misery than any other.

At least 1,600 years ago, Hindu physician Dhanwantari listed the symptoms of smallpox in a medical book called the *Susruta Samhita*. These symptoms included fever; pain in the body, back, and joints; cough; and loss of energy and appetite. The most distinguishing feature of smallpox was the appearance of pustules—swollen, pus-filled areas on the skin. "The pustules are red, yellow, and white," wrote Dhanwantari, "and they are accompanied with burning pain." Those who didn't die of the infection were left with deep, disfiguring scars. Medieval English physicians called these "pockes." The phrase "small pockes" was adopted to distinguish this disease from syphilis, another common illness that left larger scars.

The severity and frequency of smallpox outbreaks promoted innovative treatments. During China's Song dynasty (960–1279 CE), physicians noticed that those who survived smallpox never suffered another infection. They wondered if exposing people to a mild form of the disease would produce resistance. It was just crazy enough to work. Physicians collected scabs from the pustules of recuperating smallpox victims and blew them through a straw into the nose of a healthy person. Sure enough, the person suffered a mild form of smallpox afterward—but his or her chance of survival was far greater than without the preventive treatment.

Merchants spread this treatment west. Each culture made its own modifications. In India, physicians often made cuts on the patient's skin and placed smallpox scabs atop the wounds. Turkish doctors abandoned the scabs and instead collected fluid from smallpox pustules, rubbing a drop or two into cuts on the patient's upper arm. Dr. Emanuel Timoni observed this inoculation procedure in 1714, while he was practicing medicine in Constantinople (now the Turkish city of Istanbul). Members of London's Royal Society were doubtful when he wrote this description:

> This the Doctor attests from his own observation . . . that such as have this inoculation practiced on them, are subject to very slight symptoms, some being very scarcely sensible they are ill or sick; and, what is valued by the fair, it never leaves any scars or pits in the face.

The Battle for Inoculation

In the end, it was a determined mother who brought inoculation to Europe. Lady Mary Wortley Montagu survived smallpox in her youth, but she lost her beloved brother to the disease— and her beauty. When her husband was assigned as Britain's ambassador to the Ottoman Empire (now Turkey), Lady Mary had the opportunity to observe the practice of inoculation first-hand. She wrote to a friend:

> I am patriot enough to take pains to bring this useful invention into fashion in England; and I should not fail to write to some of our doctors very particularly about it, if I knew any one of them that I thought had virtue enough to destroy such a considerable branch of their revenue for the good of mankind.

Lady Mary not only spoke out in favor of "this useful invention" but also had her children inoculated. Britain's royal family wanted this protection for their children as well but ordered that inoculation first be tried on six prisoners, then on a group of orphans. These lower-class citizens had no choice in the matter. Fortunately, these people survived, and their immunity encouraged some physicians to proceed with inoculation. The Reverend Edmund Massey was among those who protested. Like many others, he believed that disease was a punishment for sin and the prevention of disease was up to God alone.

American minister Cotton Mather knew that most people would eventually get smallpox . He saw inoculation as a brave risk, the outcome of which would be determined by God. Mather knew nothing of the inoculation controversy underway in London, but he had read about inoculation in Royal Society publications. His former slave, Onesimus, had also revealed that a form of inoculation was successfully used in parts of Africa. In April 1721, when a smallpox epidemic began in Boston, Reverend Mather immediately began to argue for the use of inoculation. Most of the local physicians—and his fellow ministers—turned their backs on him. Dr. William Douglass suggested that this plan was as dangerous as throwing a bomb into town. James Franklin and his younger brother Benjamin Franklin used their newspaper, the *New England Courant*, to publish criticisms of inoculation.

One brave doctor agreed to stand with Mather. Zabdiel Boylston began by inoculating his young son and two slaves. The doctor had to hide from crowds eager for his blood. But Boylston and Mather soon had their reward. The three patients recovered quickly, and Boylston eventually found a total of 248 patients willing to try the procedure. Of these, only six died. Among 5,980 Bostonians who chose not to be inoculated, there were 844 deaths.

Despite high death tolls in cities around the world, the debate over the benefits and dangers of inoculation continued for decades. It would take the prominent voice of Benjamin Franklin to turn the tide of opinion in America. In 1759, twenty-three years after the death of his own son from smallpox, Franklin wrote in favor of the procedure.

Toward a More Perfect Immunity

Edward Jenner became a physician in rural England during the late eighteenth century. He often visited patients on dairy farms. It was not unusual for him to see milkmaids who had a rash on their hands. The rash was short-lived, occurring after the girls had milked cows with a similar rash on their udders. Folk stories suggested that people who experienced this cow-pox never got smallpox.

Jenner's colleagues scoffed at this idea, but he remained curious. When a patient named Sarah Nelmes reported having cowpox in 1796, Jenner seized the opportunity to conduct a test. He obtained a small amount of fluid from a pustule on Nelmes's hand and inoculated it into the arm of an eight-year-old boy named James Phipps. James became slightly ill but quickly recovered. When Jenner inoculated him with smallpox a few weeks later, he showed no reaction. To be sure that immunity was permanent, Jenner tested James Phipps many times over the years. He also repeated the experiment with other people. His results were consistent: inoculation with cowpox provided immunity to smallpox, apparently with few side effects. The Latin word for cow—*vacca*—provided the root for Jenner's new

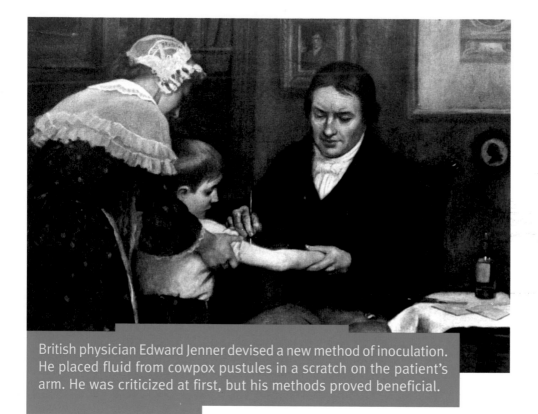

British physician Edward Jenner devised a new method of inoculation. He placed fluid from cowpox pustules in a scratch on the patient's arm. He was criticized at first, but his methods proved beneficial.

term to describe this procedure. Vaccination was different from earlier forms of inoculation because immunity was produced by exposure to a milder or different form of the disease.

Jenner wrote of his findings to the Royal Society of London, but his paper was rejected; the scientists considered his results impossible. The public harassed him, too. Disbelievers warned that by putting material from a cow into the human body, patients would become "bovinated," or cowlike. Jenner knew this was unreasonable because humans ate beef and drank cows' milk all the time without harm. Others said that his patients were nothing more than guinea pigs in a dangerous experiment. But Jenner carried on, explaining (as Mather had) that his patients were already at risk of contracting smallpox, which was far more dangerous.

A nationwide survey proved him correct. Indeed, those who had contracted cowpox were naturally resistant to smallpox. Jenner's procedure was soon adopted in Europe. Professor Benjamin Waterhouse of Harvard University brought vaccination to the United States. In 1799, Waterhouse obtained permission from President Thomas Jefferson to begin a program of cowpox vaccination in the city of Boston. Jefferson eagerly requested that his own family be vaccinated and ordered the formation of a new agency in Washington, D.C. As head of the National Vaccine Institute, Waterhouse was asked to establish a program to begin vaccinating American citizens.

The Germ Theory

The question remained: how do diseases such as smallpox spread through a population? Throughout time and in many cultures, disease has been considered a punishment from the gods. Europeans and Americans long believed that disease could result spontaneously from exposure to bad climate, food, or miasma (foul air from waste or the environment). Islamic physician and scholar al-Rāzī (865–925 CE) was among the first to propose that disease might be passed from person to person. He advised people to "keep away" from those with smallpox— "otherwise this disease might turn into an epidemic." More than six hundred years later, Italian physician Girolamo Fracastoro wrote that invisible particles might act as "seeds of infection"— lodging in clothes and bed linens, on the skin, or even passing through the air. Similar theories attracted some interest among scientists. But the average person resisted the idea that miniscule particles could exist, let alone cause deadly diseases.

An important clue was revealed in the seventeenth century, when a Dutch cloth merchant named Antoni van Leeuwenhoek began to build simple microscopes in his spare time. Through the glass of his tiny microscopes, Leeuwenhoek became the first to see organisms in pond water. He gave them a Latin name—animalcules, or little animals. In 1683, Leeuwenhoek decided to examine scrapings from his teeth. Always proud of his dental hygiene, he was morbidly fascinated to find that his teeth were home to impossibly small, rod-shaped organisms.

Experiments conducted by Louis Pasteur in the 1850s proved that animalcules could also cause disease. (He called them germs; today, scientists prefer the term "microbes.") Pasteur was asked to investigate the cause of spoilage at a vineyard. He observed samples of spoiled and unspoiled wine under the microscope. In the unspoiled wine, he identified tiny, round germs that turned out to be yeast. These caused fermentation that turned grape juice into alcohol. The spoiled wine contained rod-shaped bacteria, but little yeast. Pasteur experimented with different temperatures until he found one at which the bacteria died but the yeast lived. In the absence of bacteria, yeast populations thrived and the wine did not spoil. Pasteur's experiments established a relationship between bacteria and disease, confirming the germ theory of disease. He soon proposed that, while bacteria caused some illness, yet smaller germs—which he called viruses—must be responsible for other infectious diseases.

L.PASTEUR
1822-1895

PROCÉDÉ CAMIS Breveté

CAMIS·S.G·PARIS

French chemist Louis Pasteur discovered that microscopic organisms in the environment are among the causes of disease. Experimenting with them in the 1870s, he found that exposure to weakened bacteria and viruses could prevent disease.

The most significant development came as a surprise even to Pasteur. In 1879, he had been working to create a vaccine against chicken cholera. When his assistants mishandled the bacteria, the specimens underwent a change. Suddenly, exposed chickens sickened and recovered—much like people exposed to cowpox. Pasteur realized that the bacteria must have been weakened. He set out to make similarly weakened vaccines against anthrax, a type of bacteria known to kill sheep. Next, he tackled rabies, a deadly virus that is passed to humans through animal bites. In 1885, he had a chance to try out the rabies vaccine on a young boy named Joseph Meister, who had been bitten by a rabid dog. Pasteur gave Joseph shots every day for ten days. Each shot contained a slightly stronger dose of the rabies virus. Ideally, Joseph's body would build up immunity. The boy survived, and many saw Pasteur as a savior. Others considered the trade-off a poor one. They spoke out against Pasteur for killing rabbits to make his rabies vaccine and for "poisoning the flocks and herds of France" with anthrax and other vaccines.

It has been 125 years since Pasteur created the rabies vaccine. Although vaccination is now commonplace around the world, the addition of new vaccines over time has only fueled the fire between critics and supporters.

ARE VACCINES EFFECTIVE?

Have you ever heard someone say that an illness is "going around"? A member of your family or class shows symptoms of a cold, influenza (the flu), or strep throat, and before long, you and several other people are also feeling sick. The illness may even become an epidemic, appearing among people in the wider community. This does not happen with asthma or diabetes. Such diseases occur in families and communities, but you can't catch them from another person.

Infectious diseases are caused by pathogens—bacteria, viruses, fungi, and protozoa (single-celled, animal-like organisms). Similar microbes are all around us. Many are harmless, and some do good work. For example, certain bacteria decompose organisms after death, while others convert chemicals into useful nutrients in soils and water. In your

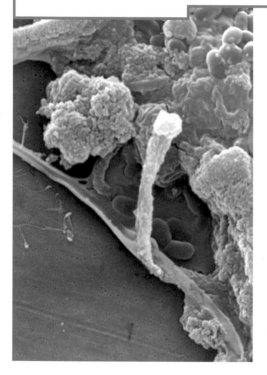

Microbes are common in our environment. Some cause disease, while others are beneficial. This image was taken with a powerful scanning electron microscope. It shows bacteria, amoebae, and other microbes in water from a stream.

body, microbes may provide services such as helping to digest food. Only those that cause disease are called pathogens. When you cough or sneeze, pathogen-filled fluids are dispersed into the air. People close by may breathe in these particles; they may also touch surfaces contaminated by the airborne particles. Bodily fluids such as blood or waste (like urine or feces) can also contain pathogens. These can be transmitted to surfaces when people fail to wash their hands after using the restroom. Historically, sewage leaks were one of the most common routes for the spread of infectious disease.

How Do We Fight Pathogens?

Your body has numerous defenses to block the invasion of pathogens. Skin is the first barrier. Saliva contains an acidic chemical that can dissolve pathogens. Microbes that enter the nasal passages are usually caught in sticky mucus. Passageways to the lungs are lined with hairlike cilia that trap particles. If sneezing doesn't expel this material, it is coughed back into the throat and swallowed, allowing digestive acids in the stomach to do their work.

Pathogens that penetrate these defenses can begin to spread through the blood or infect tissues of the body. The body's immune system response is more complex than the battle plan of a large army. Imagine that you have just been exposed to rubella, the virus commonly called German measles. As the virus begins to move through your system, it is first identified by large white blood cells called macrophages. Like guards on patrol, these cells constantly circulate through the bloodstream in search of pathogens. Macrophages consume as many rubella viral units as possible, but they also take pieces of the pathogen back to the nearest lymph node.

The outer coating, or antigen, of every pathogen is unique. Two types of lymphocyte cells learn the shape of the antigen. T cells seek out and destroy your own body cells that have already been infected with the virus. Meanwhile, B cells produce antibodies that match the shape of the antigen. Antibodies cover the surface of the virus, blocking it from entering your healthy cells. This response takes a few days, so the virus has time to reproduce and cause illness. You may experience low-grade fever, swollen glands in the throat, and a rash that starts on the face. When you recover, you will have a lasting supply of immune cells capable of rapidly recognizing and fighting this virus. You will have become immune to rubella.

Recovering from an infectious disease often provides natural immunity. A baby may gain passive immunity by receiving antibodies from the mother's bloodstream. Vaccines provide artificial immunity by introducing dead or weakened pathogens into the body. Macrophages and lymphocytes respond to vaccines as they would to any pathogen. Afterward, the body has immunity and can prevent an infection from developing.

How Are Vaccines Made?

Pathogens are grown in laboratories and go through numerous stages to produce a vaccine. First, the pathogen is treated so that it is unable to cause infection. This can be done in several ways. In some cases, pathogens are inactivated or "killed" by exposure to a chemical or heat. If you receive a seasonal flu injection, it was made this way. Although inactivated viruses are unable to reproduce and therefore cannot cause illness, the immune system still responds and produces antibodies. Attenuated vaccines are those containing live pathogens that have been weakened or changed in some way. One example is the seasonal flu nasal spray vaccine. MMR, a combined vaccine containing measles, mumps, and rubella, is also attenuated. Like inactivated vaccines, attenuated vaccines are unable to reproduce. Healthy people typically respond well to them, but people with weak immune systems may develop symptoms like the disease.

Two types of vaccine use only parts of the pathogen. Researchers have found that in some cases, antigens are suffi-

One important aspect of vaccine production is testing. Scientists regularly look at samples of pathogens to see whether they have changed. If so, vaccines must be modified to improve their effectiveness.

cient to prompt an immune response. Because subunit vaccines are not complete pathogens, they cannot cause disease. Hepatitis B is a subunit vaccine that is composed of only the surface proteins of the virus. Researchers can also extract the toxic chemicals made by some pathogens. These types of vaccines are used in cases where the toxin, rather than the microorganism itself, causes illness. After treatment with chemicals, these are harmless. But the immune system recognizes toxoids as foreign substance and creates antibodies. Tetanus is a toxoid.

Other forms of vaccine are still being developed. DNA vaccines would introduce segments of DNA from a pathogen into the body. Human cells could use this DNA to produce antigens, promoting an immune response. In a recombinant vector vaccine, the DNA of one pathogen is inserted into a different pathogen that has been attenuated or killed. The second pathogen carries the first into the body.

After a pathogen has been treated, it is mixed with other fluids and chemicals. Preservatives defend the vaccine from contamination by other pathogens and make it last. Adjuvants boost the immune system's response to the vaccine, increasing its effectiveness. Each batch of vaccine is tested for effectiveness and to assure that it is not contaminated. The approved product is packaged into vials or syringes and sent out to hospitals and clinics.

What Really Prevents Disease?

In 1999, the Centers for Disease Control and Prevention (CDC) listed vaccination first among public health achievements of the twentieth century. The National Institute of Allergy and Infectious Diseases reported that, during the past century, nine of the most common infectious diseases affecting U.S. citizens have declined dramatically. Americans are 95 percent less likely to contract measles, mumps, rubella, *Haemophilus influenzae* type B (Hib), or tetanus. Smallpox has been completely eradicated, and polio is close to this point. In locations such as Africa and the Middle East, infectious diseases are far more common. As a result of vaccination programs, the Global Health Council reported that deaths from

Florence Nightingale saw the terrible conditions in European army hospitals. Injured soldiers were exposed to dirt, disease, and hunger. Nightingale returned to England and began a campaign to make hospitals safer for patients.

measles have declined by 90 percent since 2000.

Others believe that infectious disease has been controlled by improvements in hygiene and sanitation, not by vaccination. English nurse Florence Nightingale was the first to emphasize rigorous hygiene in hospitals as a way to reduce infections. In the 1860s, Scottish physician Joseph Lister ordered all surgical instruments and wounds to be cleaned with a solution of carbolic acid. Deaths from infection declined noticeably. Although Pasteur supported vaccination, he was also convinced that hygiene and sanitation play a key role in preventing disease.

Although European physicians continued to debate the role of germs in causing disease, hygiene practices became increasingly more common in hospitals. In time, families, schools, and businesses also adopted the practice of maintaining a clean environment, and individuals began maintaining clean bodies, covering coughs, and staying at home when ill in order to prevent the spread of disease.

At the same time, public health officials were beginning to recognize the potential for water and sewage to spread disease. In 1854, during an outbreak of cholera in London, English physician John Snow traced cases of the disease to a well that had been contaminated with human waste. Britain soon set up water filtration systems. These eventually became common in the United States and elsewhere. Sewage treatment systems that removed bacteria and other pathogens followed, further reducing the risk of infectious disease.

Balance Equals Success

Despite exceptional advances in modern medicine, infectious diseases remain common in the poorest regions of the world. According to the World Health Organization (WHO), in 2005, about 2.6 billion people lacked access to clean water or sewage systems. These people are vulnerable to a wide variety of infectious diseases, which cause about 4,500 deaths per day. Children under the age of five are especially at risk because they may be severely malnourished and therefore unable to resist infections.

Which would solve this problem more effectively: proper sanitation or vaccination? This is like asking if the chicken came before the egg. Both efforts are costly and challenging. This may be a case that calls for balance. Increased efforts at building infrastructure—the systems and services that provide clean water and sewage—can improve living conditions and reduce exposure to pathogens. Education may help people learn how to maintain the quality of their improved environment. Vaccination provides protection against common, devastating diseases that spread between people.

No vaccine can provide perfect immunity. Physicians and public health officials understand this, and so should you. Each person responds uniquely to vaccines, just as he or she develops natural immunity in different ways. You may develop strong immunity to a vaccine, while your best friend does not respond at all. Another person may experience side effects to the procedure or even have a severe allergic reaction. Physicians and families must weigh these risks against the effectiveness of vaccines in preventing disease.

chapter three

HOW MANY VACCINES ARE THERE?

Louis Pasteur's development of the rabies vaccine in 1885 set off a landslide of vaccine research. Within half a century, vaccines had been produced for ten of the world's most threatening infectious diseases, including plague, diphtheria, and tuberculosis. Together, vaccination and hygiene programs increased the quality of life of people in many parts of the world. People could also hope to live longer as a result of improvements in medicine. In 1900, the average American man had a life span of 46.3 years. By 1950, this number had increased to 65.6 years. The average female life span was almost five years longer.

Despite these successes, waves of infectious disease continued to take lives worldwide. During World War I, a pandemic (global epidemic) of influenza caused approximately twenty-five million deaths. Soon after, a bacterial infection called typhoid fever killed more than

The influenza pandemic of 1918 caused such a high death rate that people lived in constant fear of catching the disease. These Seattle police officers wear masks to protect them while they work.

three million people in Europe. In the summers of 1952 and 1953, ninety thousand children were hospitalized with poliovirus, which left many paralyzed. The rubeola virus, sometimes called measles, remained a curse for children around the world until the 1960s.

Ready for School?

In order to reduce the spread of infectious diseases, particularly among children, U.S. public health officials in the 1960s decided to develop a vaccination schedule. Their first priorities were the eradication of smallpox and polio. Over time, more vaccines became available and were added to the list. Although the federal government has never required any vaccines, states have increasingly used the schedule to determine which vaccines must be given before students can enter kindergarten. Proof of vaccination may also be linked to families' ability to receive federal and state welfare funding and other services.

Ten vaccinations are currently on the school list in most U.S. states. These cover the diseases shown to cause the greatest health risk or those that result in the most school absences among children. These vaccinations are for:

Diptheria. This is a bacterial infection that affects the respiratory system. It can spread to the heart and nervous system.

Tetanus. This disease is sometimes called lockjaw. These bacteria are common in soil but also occur in animals and waste. They enter the body through wounds, causing muscle spasms and eventually locking the jaw closed. Although tetanus is an uncommon infectious disease, the CDC reports that one in ten infections results in death.

Pertussis. Better known as whooping cough, this is a highly contagious bacterial infection. It produces violent coughing that can lead to vomiting and weight loss. Pertussis usually doesn't cause death directly, but it can lead to pneumonia. It is particularly serious in infants.

Polio. Poliovirus is unpredictable. Some people show no symptoms, while others experience paralysis after the virus enters the nervous system. Death may occur if the lungs are affected.

Haemophilus influenzae type b (Hib). This can cause bacterial meningitis, an infection that targets the spinal cord and brain, and pneumonia (lung infection) and epiglottitis (a severe throat infection). Children under the age of five are especially vulnerable.

Rubeola. Otherwise known as measles, this is an extremely contagious virus that causes coldlike symptoms and a rash. Serious cases of measles can permanently damage the ears or lead to pneumonia, brain damage, or death.

Mumps. This is also a viral infection. The most obvious symptom is swelling of the cheeks and neck. It sometimes leads to deafness or meningitis and, rarely, death.

Rubella. Sometimes called German measles, this is usually a mild viral infection. But miscarriages and birth defects may occur among pregnant women who contract rubella, and women are vulnerable to arthritis after infection.

Hepatitis B. This virus affects the liver and can lead to permanent liver damage or cancer, especially in adults.

Varicella. More commonly called chickenpox, this is generally considered a mild viral infection. The rash may produce skin infections, and rare severe cases can lead to pneumonia. A risk of varicella is the development of shingles in adulthood. This rash is accompanied by severe pain.

Several of these vaccines are routinely given in combination—as a shot including several vaccines together. For example, diphtheria, tetanus, and pertussis are usually combined in a vaccine called DTaP. MMR contains measles, mumps, and rubella vaccines. Requirements for dosage vary by state. Commonly,

In 1995, then-First Lady Hillary Clinton and Dr. Henry Foster visited a childcare center in Washington, D.C., to promote National Infant Immunization Week.

states require kindergarteners to have five doses of DTaP, four of polio, and three to prevent hepatitis B. Students also need two vaccinations each against MMR and varicella, plus one to prevent Hib.

Some vaccines require later booster shots to provide complete immunity. The Tdap is a shot commonly given to adolescents aged eleven to eighteen as a booster for tetanus, diptheria, and pertussis.

Many insurance plans cover routine vaccinations. However, lower-income Americans who have no insurance may feel overwhelmed by the cost. This should never be a reason to miss vaccinations. The Comprehensive Childhood Immunization Act of 1993 guarantees free vaccinations to eligible children. If your family would benefit from this assistance, check with your local health department for information about clinics offering the service.

Do I Have To?

The childhood vaccine schedule includes a number of other vaccines that are not required for children to enter U.S. kinder-gartens. The pneumococcus vaccine is given to infants because these bacteria infect people with weak immune systems. It can lead to meningitis, blood infections, or pneumonia—all of which may be life-threatening. Meningococcus bacteria are more rare, but active infections spread very quickly, especially in daycare centers. Risks are similar to those from pneumococcal infection.

The influenza virus is probably familiar to most people. It causes respiratory symptoms that may come with high fever. The flu cough is miserable and can linger for weeks after other symptoms have disappeared. Many people are not aware that this virus sickens millions of people and causes twenty thousand to fifty thousand deaths each year in the United States alone. Because the virus evolves over time, people have to be inoculated each year with the strains and types that are estimated to be circulating.

The newest vaccines were approved for use in 2006. Rotavirus infects the intestines, causing severe diarrhea and fever. This virus is so widespread that researchers suggest most children have had it by the age of five. Infection generally passes in about a week, although about 2 percent of children may require hospitalization. The number of rotavirus cases declined dramatically in just a year after the vaccine was introduced.

The human papillomavirus (HPV) is quite different from other vaccine-prevented diseases because it is primarily transmitted through sexual contact. It is estimated to infect six million Americans each year, leading to cervical cancer in about 10,000 women and about 3,700 deaths per year. The HPV vaccine series has been recommended for girls beginning at age nine to thirteen.

An increasing number of parents are concerned that the list of recommended vaccines has grown too large. They notice that new vaccines don't always focus on protecting against life-threatening or widespread diseases. Some opponents say that these vaccines are just a way for manufacturers to make money. There are charges against specific vaccines as well. It has been argued that the rotavirus vaccine is designed to aid parents who don't want to care for a sick child. (This vaccine may be more crucial in developing nations, where diarrhea is the number-one cause of death among young children.)

The HPV vaccine has been criticized for several reasons. Some critics believe that a vaccine against a sexually transmitted disease may give approval for teenagers to be sexually active. Concerns have also been raised that the HPV vaccine has not been researched long enough to understand its short-term or long-term risks. By contrast, cervical cancer has generally been easy to diagnose, and—although a serious disease—has a high rate of success in treatment. Teens and parents will have to weigh their values and concerns when asked about these new vaccines.

Adults, Too?

Right now, your parents probably make decisions about your vaccination schedule. As an adult, you will have to make these choices on your own. You may face the first of these decisions as you prepare for college. Many colleges require students to have the meningococcus vaccine if they plan to live in a dormitory. Proof of immunity to measles is also a common expectation. Your physician will probably remind you to update your tetanus shot every ten years because immunity to this bacterial infection tends to decrease over time. You may hear older family members discussing shingles. People over the age of sixty are advised to take this vaccine if they have ever had chickenpox.

If you change physicians or lose track of your immunization record, ask your parents for help. They are expected to keep track of this information. Your schools may also have a copy of the record on file. Another resource is your state health department.

Expect to take a whole new round of vaccinations if you travel outside your home country or join the military. These may include shots for typhoid, yellow fever, tuberculosis, or Japanese encephalitis. The anthrax vaccine has been given to U.S. troops off and on since the Gulf War in 1990. The military hopes it will protect them if anthrax bacteria are ever used as a weapon. Side

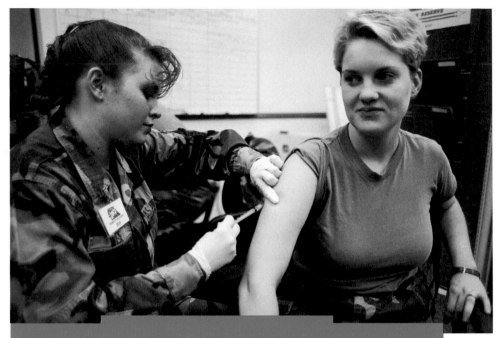

Military personnel routinely receive vaccinations before being shipped overseas. This woman is being given an injection of anthrax vaccine.

effects from the anthrax vaccination may be unusually strong in some people, but the military prefers this risk to leaving troops unvaccinated.

Whatever choices you make about vaccines, now and in the future, critics and supporters would advise you to be informed.

Ten Great Questions to Ask a Doctor

1 Which diseases can be prevented by vaccinations?

2 How many doses of each vaccine do I need?

3 What is the schedule for vaccinations?

4 Are there any circumstances under which you would advise me not to be vaccinated?

5 What side effects might I expect from this vaccination?

6 What do I do if I have severe side effects from a vaccine?

7 As an adult, how will I know when it's time to update my vaccinations?

8 Where can I find my health record if I lose it?

9 Should I choose the thimerosal-free flu shot?

10 What if my family can't afford the cost of vaccines?

chapter four

DO THE BENEFITS OF VACCINATION OUTWEIGH THE RISKS?

Childhood vaccinations have become like a rite of passage. Mothers gently hold their two-month-old infants as nurses give those first injections in the doctor's office. Children share stories with each other upon entering kindergarten, asking in hushed voices, "Did you get the shots?" Teens visit the doctor to get a last round before entering college. Many people take vaccinations for granted as a necessary and beneficial part of their health care routine. Other families are concerned about the possible health risks caused by vaccines.

Natural Is Better

Families may avoid vaccination because artificial immunity is not as effective as natural immunity. No vaccine can give the same level of immunity provided by natural

Public health officials may use advertising campaigns and other forms of media to remind parents of the importance of vaccination. The United Kingdom's Health Education Council created this poster in the 1980s.

exposure to an infectious disease. But the key lies in the word "exposure." To gain natural immunity, a person must first have the disease. Public health officials express concern that the current generation of parents doesn't understand the severity of infectious diseases. Vaccines have controlled these diseases so well, they say, that parents have not seen the suffering a serious outbreak can cause. Officials point out what can happen when vaccination levels fall. Between 1989 and 1991, the United States experienced an epidemic of measles. Approximately 55,000 people were diagnosed, and 136 died. Most of those who became ill were under the age of four and had not received their first dose of MMR vaccine, which is usually given around the first birthday.

Public health officials want families to focus on the positive outcomes of vaccination. The National Institutes of Health (NIH) report that just sixty years ago, smallpox killed fifty million people worldwide each year. The WHO's global vaccination program eliminated the disease by 1977. Poliovirus was likewise brought under control after the introduction of a vaccine in the mid-1950s. In 2009, fewer than 1,600 cases of polio were reported worldwide. Health officials credit these successes to herd immunity—the protection given when most members of a community are vaccinated. They also point out that vaccination can be significantly less expensive than hospitalization, and healthy people don't miss work or school.

The Cure Causes the Disease?

Fears about contamination began early in the days of vaccination—and often with good reason. Until the twentieth century, physicians routinely used the same lancet knife or syringe to inoculate different patients and ended up spreading other diseases in the process. More recent episodes of vaccine contamination have also shaken citizens' trust in the procedure. In 1942, more than three hundred thousand U.S. soldiers were given yellow fever vaccine contaminated with hepatitis B virus. One-sixth fell ill with the disease.

What about the risk that a vaccine could cause the disease it's intended to prevent? This fear dates back to the first days of inoculation, when a small amount of smallpox fluid was used to inoculate. A more recent example comes from the mid-1950s. Vaccine manufacturer Cutter Laboratories mistakenly released a batch of polio vaccine containing about 220,000 doses of live virus. At least seventy thousand people became ill with polio, a virus that affects the nervous system. Of these, 164 became severely paralyzed, and ten died.

Today, most reactions come from products' allergens (such as egg) that are added to the vaccine, rather than from the pathogen itself. Still, it's worth paying attention when you are offered a live, attenuated vaccine. These are most similar to the pathogens that we naturally encounter, so they prompt the strongest immune response and produce the most lasting immunity. But because they have not been killed, these pathogens have been known to change in the lab and become infectious. Attenuated vaccines must also be refrigerated to prevent spoilage. All vaccine manufacturers, distributors, and providers have to keep a close eye on the temperature of their supplies. But it's especially challenging to deliver vaccines to hot and distant locations where electricity is unreliable. In 2010, scientists at England's Oxford University announced a breakthrough technique in which a vaccine was mixed with sugar and dried. In this form, the vaccine could be stored for up to six months and maintained at temperatures up to 113 degrees Fahrenheit (45 degrees Celsius). By removing the need for refrigeration, this approach could make live, attenuated vaccines safer and less expensive.

Is This Normal?

After any vaccination, you may experience side effects: low-grade fever (below 100.3°F, or 38°C); mild soreness, redness, or swelling at the injection site; or irritability, for example. But these side effects should be short-term, lasting just a

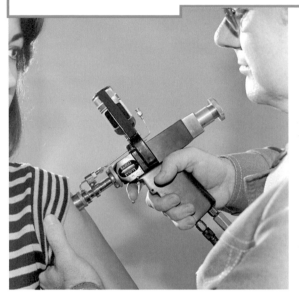

This jet injection gun uses pressure instead of a needle to deliver a vaccination. A cylinder containing gas or air pushes a stream of vaccine through the skin at such high speed that it's painless!

day or so. Much more rarely, people experience a severe allergic reaction, or anaphylaxis. Anaphylaxis is not a response to the vaccine itself but to some ingredient mixed with it. For example, MMR and some influenza vaccines may be grown inside chicken eggs. If you have an egg allergy, these vaccines could set off the allergy.

Another vaccine reaction is called Guillain-Barré syndrome (GBS). GBS attacks the spinal cord, causing muscle weakness and paralysis. In 1976, a small but significant number of people were diagnosed with GBS after receiving the swine flu vaccine. Since then, a similar reaction has occurred in some young people who received the meningococcal vaccine. Although many patients eventually recover from GBS, the symptoms are frightening.

Vaccines have been linked to a variety of other health risks, including sudden infant death syndrome (SIDS) and multiple sclerosis. SIDS occurs among babies under the age of one year. Death occurs while the child is sleeping, with no apparent cause. Some believed that the pertussis vaccine was to blame. Until 1991, the pertussis vaccine contained whole, inactivated bacteria. While most children experienced typical side effects, some had severe reactions, including high fever and convulsions. Research was not able to prove a connection between pertussis and SIDS, but a new form of the vaccine has since been developed. This subunit vaccine has fewer side effects. For whatever reason, cases of SIDS have declined by half since 1990.

Multiple sclerosis (MS) is an autoimmune disease in which the immune system attacks the insulating material covering nerves in the brain and spinal cord. While MS is not common among children, a rash of cases were diagnosed in the United States and Europe in the late 1990s. Some researchers linked these to hepatitis B vaccinations, which are given to children beginning at two months of age. Further studies failed to prove this connection, but the association has remained in parents' minds.

Such reactions spark concerns that vaccines may overwhelm a young child's immune system. Babies and toddlers routinely get four to six shots during their well-child visits. This list may include combination vaccines such as MMR and DTaP, each of which contains three vaccines. How can a little body handle such an onslaught? Physicians look to the immune system itself for answers. Small children encounter new microbes every day. Some microbes are harmless and will prompt no response;

others are pathogens that the immune system must work to defeat. All of this benefits the child, building his or her immunity for future exposures. Most physicians feel that receiving numerous vaccines adds no more stress to the body than dealing with other microbes in the environment.

Chemical Additives: A Benefit or a Threat?

Throughout the twentieth century, autism was a rare diagnosis, affecting fewer than five of every ten thousand American children. This developmental disorder seemed to strike suddenly. Young children lost their ability to speak in full sentences and began to refuse physical contact. They might sit and stare for long periods, or endlessly spin themselves or objects. In the 1990s, U.S. pediatricians noticed an increase in the number of autism cases. This trend has continued. The CDC reports that approximately 1 in 150 children now have some form of autism.

Many parents of children with autism noticed that the symptoms appeared after their children received the MMR vaccine. Scientists said this pattern was coincidental because certain medical or psychological disorders typically appear at the same age that vaccines are given. But parents were deeply concerned about their children. Some began to refuse the MMR vaccine. Others began vocal campaigns against vaccines in general.

Along the way, a new idea emerged: some children might be sensitive to chemical components in vaccines. Parents began to look at thimerosal, a mercury-based preservative developed in the 1930s to prevent vaccine contamination by bacteria and fungi. Some forms of mercury cause damage to the nervous system and learning delays in children. Thimerosal breaks down to ethyl mercury. Multiple studies show that this form of mercury leaves the body in about a month with no harmful after-effects. The risk was still too much for some parents, who began to avoid vaccinating their children. In response, the U.S. Food and Drug Administration (FDA) ordered that childhood vaccines should contain "no thimerosal or only trace amounts" (1 microgram or less per dose). Currently, the only vaccine containing larger amounts of thimerosal is the seasonal flu injection. Children five years and older can take an alternative product called FluMist that meets FDA recommendations for thimerosal.

Other vaccine chemicals add to parents' worries as well. Adjuvants are substances used to increase the immune system's response to the vaccine. Adjuvants work in different ways. For example, they sometimes act like macrophages by delivering vaccine antigens to the lymph nodes so that lymphocytes can more quickly begin making antibodies. By adding an adjuvant, more vaccine can be made from the same amount of pathogen. This could potentially help prevent vaccine shortages.

A mix of water and oil has proven effective as an adjuvant in seasonal flu vaccines. But only one chemical has been approved as an adjuvant in the United States. Alum is a salt of the metal aluminum. It is added to vaccines for hepatitis A and B, Hib, DTaP, and pneumococcus. Concerns have been raised about this choice because aluminum is known as a toxic metal. Health officials reply that alum is used at very low levels in vaccines and say that most of it leaves the body in two weeks. However, any aluminum that remains may be absorbed into the bones, lungs, and brain. Children can accumulate the metal from vaccines and other sources (such as food, breast milk, and baby formula). Most adults have a small amount of this metal stored in their bodies. Many people argue that at high levels it can cause bone degeneration, anemia (low blood count), and brain damage.

Worth the Risk?

The National Institutes of Health assure that serious reactions take place, on average, after only 1 in 100,000 vaccinations. The NIH and other health organizations emphasize that the risk of health problems from infectious diseases is far greater than the likelihood of a severe reaction. For example, the CDC reports that each year, 5 to 20 percent of the U.S. population gets sick with the influenza virus. On average, this infectious disease results in two hundred thousand hospitalizations and thirty-six thousand deaths. When a new strain of swine flu (now called H1N1) emerged in Mexico City in April 2009, it immediately sparked a debate about vaccination. Within just a few weeks, the disease had spread to almost two dozen countries. But the ghost of Guillain-Barré syndrome returned, along with other fears, and many Americans were afraid to take the vaccination. In a February 2010 report, the WHO reported that H1N1 had cost almost 16,000 lives in 212 countries.

Ongoing concerns about the safety of vaccines merit attention. In 1986, the National Childhood Vaccine Injury Act was passed.

An epidemic of swine flu broke out in Mexico City in April 2009. The situation was reminiscent of the 1918 influenza pandemic. People began wearing masks when they left home as protection from the virus.

Its major goals were to monitor the safety of existing vaccines, fund the research and development of new vaccines, and make sure that vaccine supplies remain high. Another priority of the act was to investigate possible cases of injury from vaccines. The Vaccine Adverse Events Reporting System (VAERS) collects information about side effects that may be linked to vaccination. Any person, including physicians and individuals, can report an incident to VAERS. A companion program, called the National Vaccine Injury Compensation Program, allows Americans to apply for payment if they experience severe side effects from vaccines.

Myths and Facts

All vaccines contain mercury preservatives.

Fact ➡ In response to parental concerns, the U.S. government ordered a phaseout of thimerosal, a mercury-based preservative that was once widely used in vaccines. Since 2001, children's vaccines have been made without thimerosal or contain only traces of the preservative. To learn more about thimerosal in vaccines, search the U.S. Food and Drug Administration's Web site or ask your doctor.

Receiving several vaccinations at once is stressful to a child's immune system.

Fact ➡ Children are exposed to new microbes—including pathogens—every day. The immune system is designed to tackle these. The addition of a few new pathogens from vaccination has not been proved to cause illness or make vaccine side effects more powerful.

Infectious diseases are so well controlled by vaccination that some parents can safely choose not to have their children vaccinated.

Fact ➡ Infectious diseases still exist in the population and in different parts of the world. As a result, infectious diseases emerge when people become lax about vaccination. Travelers can also carry pathogens from country to country. But many public health officials agree with parents on this matter, saying, "It is still reasonable to ask whether it's really worthwhile to keep vaccinating." Information is the key to making good decisions.

chapter five

SHOULD VACCINATION BE MANDATORY?

In 1800, Britain's army and navy prepared to battle troops led by French general Napoleon Bonaparte. But Napoleon's war was not the only thing they feared. Epidemics of smallpox were a constant threat in Europe at the time. Frederick Augustus, Duke of York, ordered that all of his soldiers be vaccinated against smallpox before leaving to fight. This was the first time that vaccination was required for any group of citizens.

The Law of the Land

Vaccination laws soon became common in Europe and the United States. The king of Wittenberg, a region that is now part of eastern Germany, declared in 1818:

Every child must be vaccinated before it has completed its third year . . . No person to be received into any school,

Frederick Augustus, Duke of York (in central England), may have saved the lives of many of his soldiers by having them vaccinated before they went to war. Smallpox often spread among the troops.

college, or charitable institution; be bound apprentice to any trade; or hold any public office who has not been vaccinated.

The U.S. city of Boston passed a similar law in 1827, requiring students attending public schools to show that they had been vaccinated against smallpox. Parents tended to follow the law more closely when epidemics came to town and ignored it in healthier times. The city found it hard to agree on whose job it was to design and enforce the vaccination law. School boards felt they had the right as leaders of the educational community, while health boards wanted control because they knew more about the disease. Without a clear strategy to follow, nineteenth-century Boston schools sometimes wound up simply taking the word of parents about whether their children had been vaccinated or not.

Legal battles began almost as soon as vaccine laws were passed. In an early case in Vermont, a citizen sued his town to pay for vaccination for all citizens. The state supreme court supported his case. When a school vaccination case came before the Pennsylvania Supreme Court in 1894, the justices stated that the government's job was not to evaluate public opinion of vaccination. More important, they said, was to use the best available medical information to make decisions about protecting public health.

The U.S. Supreme Court heard another important case in 1905 after Massachusetts gave its local health boards the power to order vaccinations. Henning Jacobson, of Cambridge, Massachusetts, refused to obey. He argued that mandatory vaccination violated "the right of every freeman to care for his own body and health in such a way as to him seems best." The court said that in certain situations, public good outweighs personal liberty. But it stressed that the government's power to make decisions should only be used when necessary and by methods that are appropriate to the situation. (For example, entering someone's house without permission to give vaccinations would not be appropriate.) The decision also stated that vaccination cannot be required if a person may experience undue harm from the procedure—for example, if the individual is allergic to any ingredient in the vaccine.

I Protest

Today, a variety of arguments are used against mandatory vaccination. Many are based on concerns about health risks. Others center on the same issues raised in those early legal cases. Critics

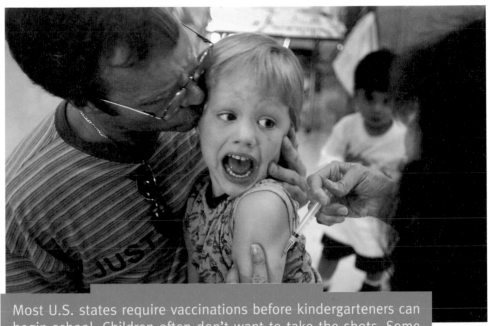

Most U.S. states require vaccinations before kindergarteners can begin school. Children often don't want to take the shots. Some parents may be concerned about side effects or feel that health decisions should be made within the family.

may feel that mandatory vaccination deprives them of civil liberties that are promised in the U.S. Constitution. Like Henning Jacobson, they believe that the right to privacy allows each person to make choices about health care without interference from the government. Parents may also feel that school vaccination conflicts with their religious beliefs. They may refer to the First Amendment of the Constitution, which guarantees the right to religious freedom.

If your family has a sincere religious conflict with vaccination, most states offer a religious exemption. This allows you to skip school vaccinations, but it usually requires proof of involvement with certain churches known to have such beliefs. A few states offer exemptions for moral or other personal reasons. One concern has been that some parents use these exemptions even though they do not meet the criteria. Another concern is that under-immunized children could potentially lead to outbreaks of disease, hence infringing on the rights of others to live a healthy life.

Do laws always get the best results? Some people respond well to them. But laws always provoke resistance, just as rules do in families. In truth, it's not clear if school vaccination laws are totally responsible for the dramatic declines in infectious diseases over the past half-century. A number of other efforts have been used to promote vaccination over this same period, and it's almost impossible to tease apart their effects. Public education programs have informed families about the benefits of vaccination and the risks of infectious disease. People have become more informed about hygiene as well.

Two Points of View, One Decision

In every community, there are some who question the requirement to vaccinate. Perhaps you have already formed an opinion. If not, you may feel conflicted by the variety of information from both sides of the debate:

The public health official says: vaccination is one of the most cost-effective public health strategies available. Maintaining a high level of herd immunity is crucial to blocking future outbreaks of infectious disease. It's best for the government to determine a vaccination schedule for all citizens to follow. This includes mandating vaccinations that children will have before entering school and requiring vaccination for citizens who join the military and receive government welfare funds. Taking vaccinations is important not only to protect your health and the health of your child, but also to keep our society healthy.

The vaccine critic counters with: vaccination exposes people, especially children, to a variety of potential health risks that have not been thoroughly explored by medical researchers. There are too many vaccines on the schedule, and several are for diseases that are not life-threatening. Childhood diseases may be so well controlled by voluntary vaccination and hygiene that mandatory vaccination is no longer necessary. Regardless, the government should not make laws regarding personal health care. Instead, physicians should provide better information about the risks and benefits of vaccination and allow individuals to choose.

The decision often depends on perspective. An individual weighs risks to his or her own health; parents prioritize the health of their children. Governments and public health organizations seek ways to protect the population as a whole. Looking at the question from the other side of the fence can be difficult, but it is always enlightening. Are vaccines a blessing or a curse? The debate continues.

Glossary

adjuvant A substance that boosts the immune system's response to a vaccine.

anaphylaxis A severe allergic reaction.

antibody A protein produced by the immune system that can fight antigens.

antigen The outer surface of a pathogen.

attenuate To weaken or change, as in a pathogen being prepared for a vaccine.

booster A repeat dose of a vaccine, given to renew immunity.

epidemic A disease that spreads among members of a community.

herd immunity The protection given when most members of a community are vaccinated.

immunity The body's ability to resist disease.

infectious The ability of a disease to spread.

inoculation A procedure in which patients are exposed to a substance that can produce immunity.

lymphocyte A type of cell in the immune system that produces antibodies.

macrophage A large white blood cell that consumes pathogens.

miasma Foul air from waste or the environment, once thought to cause disease.

microbe A microscopic organism.

pandemic An epidemic that spreads between countries.

pathogen A microbe that can cause disease; examples include bacteria, viruses, fungi, and protozoa.

pustule A swollen, pus-filled area on the skin seen in patients with pox viruses.

subunit A piece of something, as in a segment of pathogen antigen.

toxoid A toxin extracted from a pathogen and made inactive by chemical treatment.

vaccination Immunity produced by exposure to a mild or altered form of an infectious disease.

vaccine A substance that can produce immunity.

Caring for Children
Canadian Paediatric Society
2305 St. Laurent Boulevard
Ottawa, ON K1G 4J8
Canada
(613) 526-9397
Web site: http://www.caringforkids.cps.ca
Developed by the Canadian Paediatric Society, Caring for
    Children provides health education and information
    for families.

Institute for Vaccine Safety
Johns Hopkins Bloomberg School of Public Health
615 N. Wolfe Street, Room W5041
Baltimore, MD 21205
Web site: http://www.vaccinesafety.edu
The institute collects research on all aspects of vaccines,
    including adverse events, to educate physicians, parents,
    and the media.

Public Health Agency of Canada
130 Colonnade Road A.L. 6501H
Ottawa, ON K1A 0K9
Canada

Web site: http://www.phac-aspc.gc.ca

The Public Health Agency of Canada works to promote health, prevent chronic and infectious disease, and educate Canadians about healthy lifestyles.

U.S. Centers for Disease Control and Prevention (CDC)

1600 Clifton Road

Atlanta GA 30333

(800) 232-4636

Web site: http://www.cdc.gov

The mission of the CDC is "health promotion, prevention of disease, injury and disability, and preparedness for new health threats."

Vaccine Adverse Event Reporting System

P.O. Box 1100

Rockville MD 20849-1100

(800) 822-7967

Web site: http://www.vaers.hhs.gov

VAERS collects information about the side effects of vaccines used in the United States.

Vaccine Education Center at the Children's Hospital of Philadelphia

34th Street and Civic Center Boulevard

Philadelphia, PA 19104

(215) 590-1000

Web site: http://www.vaccine.chop.edu

The Vaccine Education Center provides public information about vaccine schedules, safety, and more.

Web Sites

Due to the changing nature of Internet links, Rosen Publishing has developed an online list of Web sites related to the subject of this book. This site is updated regularly. Please use this link to access the list:

http://www.rosenlinks.com/faq/vac

For Further Reading

Alter, Judy. *Vaccines* (Innovation in Medicine). Ann Arbor, MI: Cherry Lake Publishing, 2009.

Ballard, Carol. *Fighting Infectious Diseases* (Cutting Edge Medicine). Milwaukee, WI: World Almanac Library, 2007.

Farrell, Jeanette. *Invisible Enemies: Stories of Infectious Disease*. New York, NY: Farrar, Straus and Giroux, 2005.

Kobasa, Paul A., ed. *Pandemics* (Library of Natural Disasters). Chicago, IL: World Book, 2008.

Lassieur, Allison. *Louis Pasteur: Revolutionary Scientist* (Great Life Stories). New York, NY: Franklin Watts, 2005.

Link, Kurt. *The Vaccine Controversy: The History, Use, and Safety of Vaccinations*. Westport, CT: Praeger, 2005.

Ollhoff, Jim. *The Flu* (A History of Germs). Edina, MN: ABDO & Daughters, 2010.

Ollhoff, Jim. *Smallpox* (A History of Germs). Edina, MN: ABDO & Daughters, 2010.

Petersen, Christine. *The Microscope* (Inventions That Shaped the World). New York, NY: Franklin Watts, 2006.

Phelan, Glen. *Killing Germs, Saving Lives: The Quest for the First Vaccines* (Science Quest). Washington, DC: National Geographic Society, 2006.

Piddock, Charles. *Outbreak: Science Seeks Safeguards for Global Health* (National Geographic Investigates). Washington, DC: National Geographic Society, 2008.

Bibliography

Allen, Arthur. *Vaccine: The Controversial Story of Medicine's Greatest Lifesaver*. New York, NY: W. W. Norton & Company, 2007.

Bardell, D. "The Roles of the Sense of Taste and Clean Teeth in the Discovery of Bacteria by Antoni van Leeuwenhoek." *Microbiological Reviews*, Vol. 47, No. 1, March 1982. Retrieved January 8, 2010 (http://mmbr.asm.org/cgi/reprint/47/1/121.pdf).

Centers for Disease Control and Prevention. "Concerns About Autism." January 15, 2010. Retrieved February 1, 2010 (http://www.cdc.gov/vaccinesafety/Concerns/Autism/Index.html).

Centers for Disease Control and Prevention. "Trends in Tuberculosis—United States, 2008." *MMMR Weekly*, March 20, 2009. Retrieved January 19, 2010 (http://www.cdc.gov/mmwr/preview/mmwrhtml/mm5810a2.htm).

Dales, L. G., et al. "Measles Epidemic from Failure to Immunize." *Western Journal of Medicine*, Vol. 159, No. 4, October 1993. Retrieved February 2, 2010 (http://www.ncbi.nlm.nih.gov/pmc/articles/PMC1022280).

Dubose, René Jules, and Thomas D. Brock. *Pasteur and Modern Science*. Washington, DC: American Society for Microbiology, 1998.

Global Health Council. "The Impact of Infectious Diseases."
2010. Retrieved February 18, 2010 (http://www.
globalhealth.org/infectious_diseases).

Glynn, Ian, and Jennifer Glynn. *The Life and Death
of Smallpox*. New York, NY: Cambridge University
Press, 2004.

Harvard University. "Contagion: Historical Views of Diseases
and Epidemics." Harvard University Library Open
Collections, 2008. Retrieved January 17, 2010 (http://
ocp.hul.harvard.edu/contagion).

Hodge, James G., Jr., and Lawrence O. Gostin. "School
Vaccination Requirements: Historical, Social, and Legal
Perspectives." February 15, 2002. Retrieved January 23,
2010 (http://www.publichealthlaw.net/Research/PDF/
vaccine.pdf).

Hopkins, Donald R. *The Greatest Killer: Smallpox in History*.
Chicago, IL: University of Chicago Press, 2002.

Kluger, Jeffrey. *Splendid Solution: Jonas Salk and the
Conquest of Polio*. New York, NY: Berkley Books, 2004.

Livi-Bacci, Massimo. "Ramses V: Earliest Known Victim?"
World Health Organization. Retrieved February 2,
2010 (http://whqlibdoc.who.int/smallpox/WH_5_
1980_p22.pdf).

Livi-Bacci, Massimo. "Return to Hispaniola: Reassessing a
Demographic Catastrophe." *Hispanic American Historical
Review*, Vol. 83, No. 1, February 2003.

National Institute of Allergy and Infectious Diseases.
"Vaccine Benefits." Retrieved February 2, 2010

(http://www3.niaid.nih.gov/topics/vaccines/understanding/vaccineBenefits.html).

Orenstein, Walter A. "The Role of Measles Elimination in the Development of an Immunization Program: Measles Resurgence 1989–1991." *Pediatric Infectious Disease Journal*, Vol. 25, No. 12, 2006. Retrieved February 13, 2010 (http://www.medscape.com/viewarticle/551272_5).

Sloane, Hans, and Thomas Birch. "An Account of Inoculation by Sir Hans Sloane, Bart. Given to Mr. Ranby, to be Published, Anno 1736. Communicated by Thomas Birch R. R. Secret R. S." *Philosophical Transactions*, Vol. 49, 1,755–1,756. Retrieved December 3, 2009 (http://rstl.royalsocietypublishing.org/content/49/516).

Stutz, Bruce. "Megadeath in Mexico." *Discover*, February 2006. Retrieved February 13, 2010 (http://discovermagazine.com/discover/2006/feb/megadeath-in-mexico).

Taubenberger, J. K., and D. M. Morens. "1918 Influenza: The Mother of All Pandemics." *Emerging Infectious Diseases*, January 2006. Retrieved February 19, 2010 (http://www.cdc.gov/ncidod/EID/vol12no01/05-0979.html).

United Nations Millennium Campaign. "End Poverty 2015." Retrieved February 2, 2010 (http://www.endpoverty2015.org).

U.S. National Library of Medicine. "Variolation." National Institutes of Health, October 18, 2002. Retrieved January 31, 2010 (http://www.nlm.nih.gov/exhibition/smallpox/sp_variolation.html).

Wehrle, Paul F. "A Reality in Our Time: Certification of the Global Eradication of Smallpox." *Journal of Infectious Diseases*, Vol. 142, No. 4, 1980.

Wellcome Trust. "New Method Makes Vaccines Stable at
    Tropical Temperatures." ScienceDaily, February 18, 2010.
    Retrieved February 18, 2010 (http://www.sciencedaily.com/
    releases/2010/02/100217142631.html).

World Health Organization. "Pandemic (H1N1) 2009—
    Update 88." February 19, 2010. Retrieved February 22,
    2010 (http://www.who.int/csr/don/2010_02_19/en/
    index.html).

World Health Organization. *Water for Life: Making It Happen.*
    Geneva, Switzerland: WHO Press, 2005.

World Health Organization. "Wild Poliovirus Weekly Update."
    February 10, 2010. Retrieved February 24, 2010
    (http://www.polioeradication.org/casecount.asp).

Index

A

anaphylaxis, 38
anthrax, 14, 31–32
antibodies, 17, 18, 41
attenuated vaccines, 18, 20, 37
autism, 40–41

B

booster shots, 28

C

Centers for Disease Control
    and Prevention, 20, 26,
    40, 41
chickenpox, 27, 28, 31
cholera, 5, 14, 22
Comprehensive Childhood
    Immunization Act of
    1993, 29
cowpox, 9–10, 11, 14
Cutter Laboratories, 36

D

diphtheria, 5, 24, 26, 27, 28,
    39, 41
DNA vaccine, 19–20
DTaP vaccine, 27, 28, 39, 41

E

egg allergies, 37, 38
epidemics, 15, 35, 46, 47
epiglottis, 27

F

Food and Drug Administration,
    41, 44

G

germ theory, 11–12, 14, 21
Global Health Council, 20
Guillain-Barré syndrome, 38, 41

H

hepatitis B, 19, 27, 28, 36, 39, 41
herd immunity, 36, 50
Hib, 20, 27, 41
HPV vaccine, 30
hygiene, 21–22, 24, 51

I

immunization records, 31, 33
influenza, 5, 15, 18, 20, 24, 29,
    38, 42
insurance plans, 28–29

J

Japanese encephalitis, 31
Jenner, Edward, 9–11

L

Leeuwenhoek, Antoni van, 12
Lister, Joseph, 21

M

measles, 18, 20, 24, 27, 28, 35,
    38, 39, 40

meningitis, 27, 29, 31, 38
miasma, 11
MMR vaccine, 18, 27, 28, 35, 38, 39, 40
multiple sclerosis, 39
mumps, 18, 20, 27, 28, 35, 38, 39, 40

N

nasal spray vaccines, 18, 41
National Childhood Vaccine Injury Act, 42–43
National Institute of Allergy and Infectious Diseases, 20
National Institutes of Health, 35, 42
National Vaccine Injury Compensation Program, 43
National Vaccine Institute, 11
Nightingale, Florence, 21

P

pandemics, 24
passive immunity, 18
Pasteur, Louis, 12–14, 21, 24
pertussis, 26, 27, 28, 39, 41
plague, 5, 24
pneumonia, 5, 26, 27, 29, 41
polio, 20, 25, 26, 28, 36–37

Q

questions to ask a doctor, 33

R

recombinant vector vaccines, 20
rotavirus, 29–30
rubella, 17, 20, 27, 28, 35, 38, 39, 40

S

sanitation, 21, 22–23
smallpox, 5–9, 11, 20, 26, 35–36, 46, 47
Snow, John, 22
sudden infant death syndrome, 38–39
swine flu, 38, 42

T

Tdap, 28
tetanus, 19, 20, 26, 27, 28, 31, 39, 41
thimerosal, 33, 40–41, 44
tuberculosis, 5, 24, 31
typhoid fever, 5, 24–25, 31

V

Vaccine Adverse Events Reporting System, 43
vaccines
  benefits vs. risks, 9, 34–43, 51
  development, 4–14
  effectiveness, 15–23
  mandatory, 25–26, 27–28, 29–32, 34, 46–51
  myths and facts, 44–45
  side effects, 33, 37–39, 43, 44
  types, 14, 18–20, 24–32
varicella, 27, 28

W

whooping cough, 26, 27, 28, 39
World Health Organization, 22, 36

Y

yellow fever, 31, 36

About the Author

Christine Petersen has had a diverse career as a bat biologist, middle school science teacher, and naturalist. Now a writer, Petersen has published more than forty nonfiction books for children and young adults. She is especially interested in writing about topics that look at the impact of science in the past, present, and future. Petersen's work has been recognized by the American Association for the Advancement of Science (AAAS), and she is a member of the Society of Children's Book Writers and Illustrators. Petersen and her family live in Minnesota.

Photo Credits

Cover www.istockphoto.com/Thinkstock; p. 5 Courtesy of WHO; p. 10 Popperfoto/Getty Images; pp. 13, 35 Science & Society Picture Library/Getty Images; p. 16 CDC/Janice Haney Carr; p. 19 CDC/Maryam I. Daneshvar, Ph.D.; p. 21 Courtesy of the National Library of Medicine; p. 25 Time & Life Pictures/ Getty Images; p. 28 Joyce Naltchayan/AFP/Getty Images; p. 32 © AP Images; p. 38 CDC/Robert E. Bates; p. 43 AFP/Getty Images; p. 47 Hulton Archive/Getty Images; p. 49 David McNew/Getty Images.

Designer: Evelyn Horovicz; Editor: Bethany Bryan;
Photo Researcher: Peter Tomlinson